FROM SLOGANS TO SYSTEMS

LANGUAGE, POWER, AND THE ARCHITECTURE OF BELIEF

BY LUXORAE™

A Guide to Reclaiming Language, Interrupting Systems, And Restoring Dignity, Sovereignty, and a Liberated Life.

COPYRIGHT PAGE

From Slogans to Systems:

Language, Power, and the Architecture of Belief

Published by **Luxorae**™ LLC
Buffalo, New York

First Edition

A paperback edition is available as:
ISBN 979-8-9947700-4-7

Published by:
Luxorae™ LLC
Buffalo, NY, USA
www.LuxoraeLife.com

Printed in the United States of America

Table of Content

Introduction

This Is Not a Motivational Book

This book was not written to inspire you.

It was written to **wake you up**—gently, honestly, and without spectacle.

For generations, many of us have been taught to survive inside systems we were never meant to question. We inherited phrases that sounded like wisdom but functioned as boundaries. We were told what was "realistic," what was "for people like us," and what was simply "how things are."

Over time, these phrases stopped sounding like ideas and started sounding like facts.

This book begins with a refusal.

A refusal to treat inherited language as untouchable.
A refusal to confuse struggle with destiny.
A refusal to mistake exhaustion for truth.

From Slogans to Systems is an invitation to examine how everyday language shapes belief, behavior, and the systems that govern our lives. It is not about blaming individuals. It is about restoring responsibility to structures, design, and power—where it belongs.

You will not find affirmations here.
You will not be promised ease without effort.
You will not be told that words magically change reality.

You *will* be asked to think more precisely.
You *will* be invited to speak more consciously.
You *will* be challenged to stop normalizing harm.

This book is a guide—not to perfection, but to clarity.
And clarity is the beginning of change.

Why This Book Exists

This book is not here to shame language.
It is here to restore responsibility to it.

We are not rejecting culture.
We are reclaiming precision.

We are not denying struggle.
We are refusing to confuse struggle with destiny.

And we are not pretending that words alone change the world.
Rather, we are insisting on the foundational truth that systems have not historically changed without shifts in how people spoke about them.

This understanding is deeply rooted in critical pedagogy. Paulo Freire described the process of *conscientização*—often translated as *critical consciousness*—as the ability to name reality accurately in order to transform it. Without this capacity, Freire argued, education becomes memorization and language becomes containment rather than liberation.

Freire's work in *Pedagogy of the Oppressed* (1970) emphasizes that liberation follows from the ability to critically examine language, power, and practice. This book extends that tradition into the everyday language we inherit and repeat—the phrases we normalize, the sayings we accept, and the beliefs we pass on without questioning.

This guide offers tools to develop that critical consciousness:
to notice inherited language, to question how words shape belief and behavior, and to practice precision—not as perfection, but as care.

Author's Note

Why I Wrote This

I wrote this book because I kept hearing the same phrases repeated—by well-meaning people, by institutions, by communities carrying generations of history—and I realized something unsettling:

Many of the sayings we call wisdom were never meant to end the conversation.
They were meant to start one.

Somewhere along the way, warnings became certainties.
Survival strategies became identities.
And language that was once meant to protect us began quietly limiting us.

This book was not written to persuade you to believe something new.
It was written to help you question what you were taught to accept without examination.

Many of the phrases we repeat daily were never meant to be truths. They were tools—shortcuts for navigating systems that demanded endurance more than understanding. Over time, repetition turned those tools into ceilings. When language goes unexamined, systems harden around it.

I am not interested in erasing culture.
I am interested in finishing the work our culture began.

This guide exists at the intersection of education, social justice, trauma-informed practice, and liberation thinking. It is grounded in research, lived experience, and deep respect for the resilience of communities that have endured far more than they were ever meant to carry.

This work is not a rejection of the past, nor an accusation of those who survived before us. It is an invitation to pause, to look again, and to reclaim meaning with care. Precision matters because language shapes what we tolerate, what we imagine, and what we build. When slogans replace thinking, responsibility dissolves. When clarity disappears, harm becomes normalized.

Chapter One begins by examining how everyday language becomes infrastructure—how phrases repeated casually can shape belief, behavior, and eventually policy. From there, we move forward together, not toward blame, but toward clarity.

If this book unsettles you, pause—but do not turn away.
Discomfort is often the sound of something important being named.

This work is for readers ready to interrupt patterns without erasing history.
For those who understand that questioning is not rebellion—it is stewardship.

Let us begin where all systems begin: with language

Chapter 1
The Language We Inherited

We were taught how to speak before we were taught how to question.

Long before we knew how systems worked, before we understood history or economics or power, we were given phrases. Short ones. Portable ones. Sayings that fit neatly into moments of fear, fatigue, laughter, or warning. They were passed down in kitchens, on porches, in classrooms, in churches, in moments of love and moments of survival.

They sounded like wisdom.

They sounded like protection.

They sounded like truth.

But most of all, they sounded *finished*—as if the thinking had already been done, as if the conclusion had already been reached, as if there was nothing left to examine.

This book begins with a simple but unsettling idea:
much of what we repeat as truth is inherited language we were rarely taught to interrogate.

Not because we were lazy.
Not because we were ignorant.
But because survival often requires speed, not analysis.

Language as Inheritance

We inherit more than genetics and traditions. We inherit *phrases*.
We inherit warnings disguised as facts.
We inherit survival strategies that harden into belief.

Sociologists and linguists have long understood that language is one of the primary ways culture is transmitted across generations (Bourdieu, 1984; Lakoff, 2004). What is less often discussed is how **language carries trauma**, compressing complex historical realities into short, repeatable statements that can be quickly deployed under stress.

When a community has had to endure:

- systemic exclusion
- economic precarity
- racialized violence
- repeated disappointment
- broken promises

language adapts.

It becomes efficient.
It becomes blunt.
It becomes protective.

But protection is not the same as liberation.

Survival Language vs. Liberation Language

Survival language helps you endure hostile conditions.
Liberation language helps you change them.

Survival language sounds like:

- "That's just how it is."
- "We've always had to struggle."
- "You gotta work twice as hard."
- "Nothing ever changes."

These phrases were not created because people lacked imagination.

They were created because imagination felt dangerous when disappointment was constant.

Trauma researchers such as Bessel van der Kolk and stress researchers such as Bruce McEwen have shown that under chronic stress, the brain prioritizes certainty over possibility. Language reflects this. Repeated phrases become emotional anchors—predictable, familiar, and stabilizing even when they are limiting.

This is not a flaw.
It is a **biological and cultural adaptation**.

But adaptations are meant to respond to conditions—not become permanent identities.

How Phrases Become Beliefs

Repetition is one of the most powerful forces shaping belief. Cognitive psychologists such as Lynn Hasher, David Goldstein, and Thomas Toppino have documented that repeated ideas become easier to accept as true. Hasher et al,,.,,, When phrases are repeated across generations, they stop sounding like opinions and start sounding like laws of nature.

This is how slogans replace analysis.

This is how warnings become fate.

This is how language stops pointing at systems and starts pointing at people.

Over time, we stop asking:

- Who created this condition?

- Who benefits from this belief?
- What would have to change for this phrase to stop being true?

And instead we say:

- "It is what it is."

That sentence alone has ended more conversations than censorship ever could.

When Respect for Elders Becomes Silence

In many cultures—especially Black communities—language inheritance is deeply tied to respect. Elders survived things we cannot imagine. Their words are treated as sacred because their survival feels sacred.

But honoring elders does not mean freezing language in place.

bell hooks reminds us that love without truth becomes domination (hooks, 1994). When phrases are passed down without context, explanation, or permission to question, they become **untouchable**, even when they no longer serve the living.

This creates a quiet contradiction:

- We honor our ancestors by repeating their words
- But we dishonor their struggle if we refuse to finish the work

Honoring survival does not require repeating limitation.

The Danger of Flattened Wisdom

Many phrases that circulate widely today were never meant to end thought.

They were meant to provoke it.

"History repeats itself" was not written to declare inevitability.
It was meant to sound an alarm.

"Nothing ever changes" was not meant to describe truth.
It was meant to express exhaustion.

"You gotta be twice as good" was not meant to glorify overwork.
It was meant to warn of unfair conditions.

These phrases originated as contextual observations, not conclusions. They emerged from lived experience, collective memory, and attempts to name harm in real time. But when context disappears, something dangerous happens.

The phrases lose their teeth and gain chains.

They stop pointing outward—toward systems, power, and accountability—and begin pointing inward. What once described conditions becomes a script for identity. What once warned of injustice becomes an explanation for why nothing should be expected to change.

Flattened wisdom does not ask questions.
It closes them.

This is how language quietly shifts from meaning-making to meaning-limiting. Not through deception, but through repetition stripped of context, history, and responsibility

Language as a Quiet Enforcer

Michel Foucault argued that power works best when it no longer needs to announce itself. Language plays a critical role in this process. When people internalize phrases that explain injustice as normal, power no longer needs to justify itself.

No policy is required if people already believe:

- "That's just how it goes."
- "This world don't owe us nothing."
- "People like us don't get that."

In these moments, language becomes a silent guardrail—keeping people within mental boundaries long after physical ones have been challenged.

This is not accidental. Nor is it mystical. It reflects structural dynamics embedded in how power operates.

What begins as inherited language does not remain neutral—over time, it shapes expectation.

References

- the Conference of Referential Validity.
- hooks, b. (1994). Teaching to Transgress.
- Foucault, M. (1977). Discipline and Punish.
- Freire, P. (1970). Pedagogy of the Oppressed.

Chapter 2
From Inheritance To Consequence

Chapter One examined how language is inherited—how phrases, sayings, and narratives are passed down with meaning intact but context often stripped away. What begins as wisdom shaped by lived experience can quietly flatten into expectation when repeated without interrogation.

Chapter Two moves deeper into that process. It focuses on what happens next: when warnings harden into certainties, when caution becomes fate, and when language that once described conditions begins to dictate them. This chapter examines how repetition turns observation into inevitability—and why that shift matters.

When Warnings Became Fate

There is a difference between a warning and a prophecy.
And somewhere along the way, we stopped telling them apart.

Warnings are meant to interrupt behavior.
Prophecies, when misunderstood, can paralyze it.

This chapter exists because too many phrases that were meant to **shake us awake** have been softened, shortened, and repeated until they sound like destiny. And destiny is a dangerous thing to believe in when the systems that shape our lives were designed by human hands.

The Slow Drift from Caution to Certainty : How Language Hardens

A warning says: *pay attention.*
A certainty says: *accept it.*

The danger is not the phrase itself.
The danger is what happens when repetition replaces examination.

Over time, many of the phrases we hear most often crossed an invisible line:

- From observation to instruction
- From caution to certainty
- From signal to sentence-ending fact

"History repeats itself."
"That's just how it goes."
"It wasn't meant for us."

These statements were not originally declarations of inevitability. They were attempts to name patterns, express fatigue, or prepare people emotionally for systems that had proven resistant to change.

But repetition without context does something subtle and corrosive. It drains urgency. It replaces responsibility with resignation. The warning becomes background noise, and the listener is left believing that no intervention is required.

How Repetition Without Context Becomes Control

Psychologists call this the **illusory truth effect**: the more often something is repeated, the more likely it is to be perceived as true, regardless of accuracy (Hasher et al., 1977).

In communities shaped by repeated harm, repetition serves a double purpose:

1. It prepares people emotionally for disappointment.
2. It quietly lowers expectations.

When language is repeated across generations—without explanation, without historical grounding, without an invitation to question—it becomes an *instruction manual for how not to hope*.

This is not because people lack vision.
It is because vision without safety feels reckless.

"History Repeats Itself" Was Never the Point

The phrase "those who do not learn history are doomed to repeat it" is often misattributed, misused, and misunderstood. It was never meant to suggest that harm is inevitable. It was meant to emphasize **responsibility**.

History does not repeat itself on its own.
Systems repeat themselves when left intact.

Policies repeat.
Power structures repeat.
Economic incentives repeat.
Narratives repeat.

And when those systems are not interrupted, the outcomes feel eerily familiar—not because history has a will of its own, but because design has consequences.

To treat repetition as fate is to absolve designers of accountability.

The Quiet Theft of Agency

When people believe that nothing changes, they stop organizing.
When people believe struggle is permanent, they stop demanding better.
When people believe exclusion is natural, they stop imagining access.

This is how slogans become tools of containment.

Sociologist Pierre Bourdieu described this as *symbolic violence*—the internalization of limits imposed by external structures, enforced not by force, but by belief.

The most effective systems do not need constant enforcement. They need agreement. And agreement is often secured through language that explains injustice as normal, expected, or unavoidable.

Exhaustion Is Not Philosophy

Many of the phrases we repeat today were born from exhaustion, not ideology.

"Nothing ever changes" is not a theory.
It is fatigue speaking.

"That's just how it is" is not wisdom.
It is grief looking for rest.

But when exhaustion is mistaken for truth, despair becomes policy.

Trauma research shows that chronic stress narrows the brain's capacity for future-oriented thinking (van der Kolk, 2014). Under sustained pressure, people prioritize predictability over possibility. Language reflects this shift.

It becomes safer to expect less than to hope and be disappointed again.

But safety is not the same as freedom.

When Language Stops Pointing at Power

Originally, many warnings pointed outward—toward systems, institutions, and decisions.

Over time, they were redirected inward.

- From "this system is unfair" to "you just have to work harder."
- From "this wasn't built for us" to "we don't get those things."
- From "this structure harms people" to "that's life."

This shift is subtle but devastating. It relocates responsibility from architects to occupants. From policy to personality. From power to perseverance.

And perseverance, when demanded endlessly, becomes exploitation.

The Cost of Calling Fate What Is Design

Design can be changed.
Fate cannot.

When people confuse the two, systems gain longevity they do not deserve.

Critical theorist Paulo Freire warned that oppression succeeds not only through force, but through the internalization of inevitability. Once people believe conditions are fixed, liberation begins to feel unrealistic—or even irresponsible.

This is why slogans that flatten complexity are dangerous. They feel wise. They feel communal. They feel familiar.

But they quietly steal the future.

Reclaiming the Warning

What if we returned these phrases to their original purpose?

What if "history repeats itself" once again sounded like an alarm?

What if it meant:

Pay attention to patterns.
Interrupt systems.
Refuse normalization.

What if "nothing ever changes" became a signal—not of resignation, but of urgency?

What if we heard it as:

Then change must be forced.
Then pressure must increase.
Then imagination must expand.

Warnings are not meant to soothe.
They are meant to provoke.

The Difference Between Knowing and Interrupting

Knowing history does not prevent harm.
Interrupting systems does.

Education that stops at awareness leaves power untouched. Awareness without action can even reinforce despair—people see the problem clearly but feel unable to move it.

This is why this book insists on precision.

It is not enough to know *what happened.*
We must understand *why it keeps happening* and *who has the power to stop it.*

Language that fails to make this distinction serves stagnation, not truth.

Closing Reflection (for the Reader)

Ask yourself:

- Which phrases have I accepted as fact rather than challenge?
- Which warnings have I mistaken for fate?
- What responsibility might return to me if inevitability were no longer an option?

History does not repeat itself because it must.

It repeats when systems are protected by silence, habit, and resignation.

And silence, too, is a language.

References

- Hasher, L., Goldstein, D., & Toppino, T. (1977). Frequency and the Conference of Referential Validity.
- Bourdieu, P. (1991). Language and Symbolic Power.
- Freire, P. (1970). Pedagogy of the Oppressed.
- van der Kolk, B. (2014). The Body Keeps the Score.
- Pierson, P. (2004). Politics in Time: History, Institutions, and Social Analysis.

Chapter 3
The Cost Of Unexamined Speech

Language does not only move through the world.
It moves through us.

It settles into posture.
It shapes expectation.
It teaches the body what to brace for.

By the time language becomes visible as belief, it has often already done its work.

How Speech Becomes Self-Instruction

Every repeated phrase is a rehearsal.

When we say:

- "That's just how it is,"
- "We don't get nice things,"
- "You can't have it all,"

we are not merely describing circumstances. We are **training ourselves**—emotionally, cognitively, behaviorally—on what not to attempt.

Cognitive science shows that language influences attention and decision-making by narrowing what the brain considers possible or worth pursuing (Lakoff & Johnson, 1980). Over time, repeated language becomes a quiet instruction manual for how much hope is "reasonable."

This is not conscious surrender.
It is learned limitation.

When Words Become Internal Policy

Institutions operate through policy.
People operate through belief.

And belief is often formed by language that feels too familiar to question.

When phrases circulate long enough, they begin to function like internal regulations:

- Don't expect too much.
- Don't get your hopes up.
- Don't imagine beyond survival.
- Don't demand what hasn't been offered.

No enforcement is required.
Compliance is voluntary—because it feels like realism.

This is what makes unexamined speech so effective.
It rarely announces itself as control.
It presents itself as wisdom..

The Body Remembers What the Mouth Repeats

Trauma does not only live in memory.
It lives in anticipation.

Neuroscience research shows that chronic stress conditions the nervous system to prioritize threat detection and predict disappointment as a form of protection (McEwen, 1998; Porges, 2011). Language reflects and reinforces this state.

Phrases that minimize expectation or normalize harm often emerge from a regulated response to instability:

- Lower expectations = fewer emotional injuries.

- Predict loss = avoid surprise.
- Normalize struggle = make pain survivable.

But what protects the nervous system in the short term can **impoverish imagination** in the long term.

The body learns to expect less.
The mind learns to ask for less.
The future quietly shrinks.

The Violence of "That's Just How It Is"

Few phrases carry more quiet harm than this one.

"That's just how it is" ends inquiry.
It dismisses responsibility.
It converts design into destiny.

Political theorist Hannah Arendt warned that evil often becomes banal—not dramatic, but routine, unexamined, and linguistically normalized (Arendt, 1963). When injustice is framed as "just how things are," it stops sounding like harm and starts sounding like weather.

Unavoidable.
Natural.
Out of human hands.

But systems are not weather.
They are choices maintained over time.

Respectability, Exhaustion, and the Price of Silence

In many marginalized communities, survival has required careful speech. Say too much and you risk punishment. Ask for too much and you risk exclusion. Expect too much and you risk disappointment.

So language learned to compress:

- Hope became quiet.
- Anger became internal.
- Imagination became private.

Sociologists describe this as **adaptive silence**—a strategy for navigating hostile environments (Scott, 1990). But when silence becomes inherited rather than situational, it transforms into self-censorship.

Eventually, people stop naming harm not because it disappears—but because language for challenging it was rarely modeled.

How Unexamined Speech Rewrites Identity

Over time, language begins to define not just what we expect, but who we believe we are.

- "We always struggle."
- "People like us don't get that."
- "That's not for us."

These phrases do more than describe conditions. They become identity statements.

Social identity theory shows that repeated narratives shape group self-concept, influencing aspiration, risk-taking, and collective behavior (Tajfel & Turner, 1979).

When limitation becomes identity, expansion feels like betrayal. Success feels suspicious. Ease feels undeserved.

This is how language polices boundaries long after physical ones are challenged.

When Wisdom Becomes a Cage

Many phrases survive because they sound wise.

They were spoken by elders.
They came from experience.
They were forged in hardship.

But wisdom without context becomes dogma.

bell hooks reminds us that tradition should be a resource—not a prison. When inherited language cannot be questioned, it becomes a ceiling disguised as protection.

The goal is not to discard wisdom.
The goal is to **complete it**.

The Emotional Cost of Saying Less Than We Mean

Unexamined speech often asks people to compress their truth.

- To soften anger.
- To downplay ambition.
- To minimize grief.
- To make peace with injustice.

Over time, this creates a quiet dissonance—the feeling that one's internal reality does not match what is spoken aloud. Psychologists have linked this kind of mismatch to increased stress, disengagement, and emotional fatigue. When people cannot name their experience accurately, their ability to change it becomes limited.
Language becomes a lid.

Awareness Is Not Enough—but It Is Necessary

This chapter is not asking for perfect language.
It is asking for **intentional language**.

We are not responsible for the phrases we inherited.
But we are responsible for deciding which ones we continue to use.

Paulo Freire describes... that critical consciousness begins when people recognize that what feels "natural" is often learned—and therefore, changeable.

Unexamined speech is not neutral.
It has a cost.

It costs imagination.
It costs agency.
It costs the future.

Closing Reflection (for the Reader)

Pause and ask yourself:

- What phrases do I repeat when I'm tired?
- What language shows up when I feel defeated?
- Which words lower my expectations without my consent?
- What might become possible if I spoke more precisely about what I want and what I deserve?

Not all silence is harmful.
But unchosen silence often is.

References (Chapter 3)

- Lakoff, G., & Johnson, M. (1980). *Metaphors We Live By.*
- McEwen, B. (1998). *Protective and Damaging Effects of Stress.*
- Porges, S. (2011). *The Polyvagal Theory.*
- Arendt, H. (1963). *Eichmann in Jerusalem.*
- Scott, J. C. (1990). *Domination and the Arts of Resistance.*
- Tajfel, H., & Turner, J. (1979). *An Integrative Theory of Intergroup Conflict.*
- hooks, b. (2000). *All About Love.*
- Hochschild, A. (1983). *The Managed Heart.*
- Freire, P. (1970). *Pedagogy of the Oppressed.*

Chapter 4
Language Is Infrastructure

We tend to think of infrastructure as concrete things.
Roads. Bridges. Buildings. Pipes. Wires.

But before any of those exist, something else is laid down first.

Language.

Language is the original infrastructure. It determines where movement is allowed, where access is restricted, and which paths are considered legitimate. Long before policies are written or budgets are passed, words decide what sounds reasonable, necessary, or excessive.

If you want to understand why a system looks the way it does, listen to how people talk about it.

The Architecture Beneath the Surface

Infrastructure shapes behavior without asking permission.

A road tells you where to drive.
A fence tells you where not to go.
A poorly lit street tells you whose safety is optional.

Language works the same way.

It creates invisible routes for thought:

- What problems deserve attention
- What solutions feel realistic
- Whose needs are prioritized
- Who is expected to adapt

This is why language cannot be considered neutral. Beyond description, it actively organizes how the world is understood and navigated.

Linguist George Lakoff argues that metaphors structure how societies reason about policy and responsibility. When poverty is framed as a personal failure, solutions focus on discipline. When it is framed as structural, solutions shift toward access, policy, and redistribution.

The words come first. The systems follow.

Framing: What Language Highlights—and What It Hides

Every system rests on a frame.

Frames answer questions before they are asked:

- Is this a problem or just "the way things are"?
- Is this a failure of individuals or institutions?
- Is this harm or inconvenience?

Consider how language frames labor.

When exhaustion is called "hustle," overwork becomes admirable.
When underpayment is called "opportunity," exploitation becomes invisible.
When insecurity is called "flexibility," precarity becomes normal.

Frames do not lie outright. They **redirect attention**.

And what we do not see, we rarely challenge.

From Words to Policy

Policy language shapes what governments are willing to do.

"Law and order" prioritizes control.
"Public safety" prioritizes protection.
"Personal responsibility" narrows solutions.
"Social responsibility" widens them.

These phrases are not interchangeable. They activate different emotional responses and justify different outcomes.

Political scientists Chong & Druckman have shown that framing determines public support for policies more reliably than facts alone. People do not vote on data—they vote on meaning.

Meaning is delivered through language.

How Language Naturalizes Inequality

One of language's most powerful functions is making design appear natural.

When inequity is described as:

- "the market"
- "human nature"
- "just how it goes"

it stops sounding like a choice.

Sociologist Pierre Bourdieu described this as *misrecognition*— when social arrangements are perceived as natural rather than constructed. Language is the vehicle that carries misrecognition from generation to generation.

Once inequality feels inevitable, resistance begins to look unreasonable.

The Myth of Neutral Language

There is no such thing as neutral language in systems shaped by power.

Every term:

- includes someone
- excludes someone
- centers something
- marginalizes something else

When institutions claim neutrality, they often mean comfort for the dominant group.

"Neutral" curricula often omit marginalized histories.
"Neutral" policies often preserve unequal outcomes.
"Neutral" standards often reflect unequal starting points.

Language that refuses to name power quietly protects it.

When Efficiency Replaces Ethics

Modern systems prize efficiency.

Efficiency sounds practical. Rational. Necessary.

But efficiency language often hides moral decisions:

- Who gets help first
- Who waits
- Who is deemed too expensive to support

When systems describe people as "costs," "burdens," or "cases," they create emotional distance that makes harm easier to justify.

Psychologists have documented how bureaucratic language reduces empathy and increases tolerance for harm by abstracting human experience (Bandura, 1999).

This is how harm becomes procedural.

Why Changing Language Is Not Cosmetic

Critics often dismiss attention to language as superficial.

"Words don't change anything," they say.
"Real change is material."

But language is how material change becomes imaginable.

No policy emerges without justification.
No system persists without explanation.
No harm continues without narrative cover.

Language tells us:

- what is possible
- what is deserved
- what is realistic
- what is excessive

Change the language, and you change the range of acceptable action.

Naming Is the First Act of Design

Before a bridge is built, it is named.
Before a law is passed, it is described.

Before a budget is approved, it is defended.

Naming is not symbolic—it is preparatory.

This is why oppressed communities have frequently fought for the right to name their reality. To name violence as violence. To name exclusion as design. To name suffering as systemic.

Audre Lorde called this the transformation of silence into language and action. Without naming, harm remains private. With naming, it becomes political.

The Responsibility of Precision

Precision is not elitism.
It is accountability.

Imprecise language allows harm to hide.
Precise language reveals structure.

When we say:

- "people are struggling" instead of "wages are insufficient"
- "mistakes were made" instead of "decisions caused harm"
- "communities are underserved" instead of "resources were withheld"

we are not being polite. We are being evasive.

Systems depend on this evasion to survive.

Closing Reflection (for the Reader)

Ask yourself:

- How is language shaping what feels normal in my world?
- What words are used to justify inequality?

- What realities are hidden behind "neutral" terms?
- What would change if language named power directly?

Infrastructure is not just concrete and steel.

It is language, repeated until it feels like truth.

And truth, when named precisely, becomes the blueprint for change.

References (Chapter 4)

- Lakoff, G. (2004). *Don't Think of an Elephant.*
- Chong, D., & Druckman, J. (2007). *Framing Theory.*
- Bourdieu, P. (1991). *Language and Symbolic Power.*
- Bandura, A. (1999). *Moral Disengagement in the Perpetration of Inhumanities.*
- Lorde, A. (1984). *Sister Outsider.*

Chapter 5
How Systems Remember

People forget.

Systems do not.

This is one of the most dangerous misunderstandings of our time: the belief that because individuals change, structures must have changed too. But systems are not governed by memory the way humans are. They are governed by **design**.

And design remembers.

Memory Without a Mind

When we think of memory, we imagine consciousness. Experience. Recall.

Systems do not need any of that.

A policy remembers by continuing to operate.
A law remembers by remaining enforceable.
A funding formula remembers by allocating the same way year after year.
A school boundary remembers by determining who gets access and who does not.

No one has to actively remember the past for its consequences to persist.

This is why inequality can survive apology.
Why harm can outlive intention.
Why injustice can feel impersonal and yet precise.

The system is not cruel.

It is consistent.

History Does Not Fade—It Accumulates

Every system carries layers.

A housing policy does not reset when it is revised.
An education system does not start fresh with a new curriculum.
An economy does not forget how wealth was accumulated.

Instead, systems **accumulate advantage and disadvantage over time**.

Political scientist Paul Pierson describes this as *path dependence*: once a system is set on a trajectory, the cost of changing direction increases with every step (Pierson, 2004). Early decisions shape future options, often long after the original context is forgotten.

This is why patterns feel stubborn.
This is why outcomes look familiar.
This is why reform without disruption rarely works.

When Outcomes Are Mistaken for Behavior

One of the most effective ways systems avoid accountability is by reframing outcomes as personal traits.

- Poverty becomes laziness.
- Incarceration becomes criminality.
- Underachievement becomes lack of effort.
- Burnout becomes weakness.

But outcomes are not behavior.
They are **signals**.

Signals of access.

Signals of investment.
Signals of exposure.
Signals of design.

When systems remember, people inherit the consequences—even if they did not participate in the original harm.

The Lie of the Clean Slate

Modern culture loves the idea of a "fresh start."

New laws.
New leaders.
New programs.
New language.

But systems do not reset simply because the narrative does.

Sociologist Eduardo Bonilla-Silva warns that colorblind or "post-racial" language often masks the continued operation of racialized systems by pretending history has ended (Bonilla-Silva, 2014).

When we declare the past over without dismantling its structures, we preserve harm while congratulating ourselves on progress.

This is how memory hides behind optimism.

The Difference Between Reform and Interruption

Reform adjusts the surface.
Interruption changes the logic.

Reform asks:

- Can this be improved?
- Can we make it more efficient?

- Can we soften the edges?

Interruption asks:

- Why was this built this way?
- Who benefits from its current design?
- What would it mean to dismantle and rebuild?

Systems do not resist reform because they are evil.
They resist because reform rarely threatens their foundation.

Why Awareness Is Not Enough

Awareness is often treated as the end of responsibility.

We know better now.
We've acknowledged the harm.

We've named the history.
But systems do not respond to awareness.
They respond to **pressure, policy, and redesign**.

Critical theorist Michel Foucault argued that power adapts rather than disappears. When language changes but structure remains, systems evolve their justifications without altering outcomes.

This is how harm survives progress.

Language as the Carrier of Memory

Systems remember through language.

Through terms that:

- justify unequal outcomes
- soften accountability
- rebrand harm as necessity

- frame exclusion as efficiency

When people repeat phrases like:

- "That's just how the system works"
- "We're doing the best we can"
- "There's no funding for that"

they unknowingly participate in the system's memory.

Language becomes the relay between past design and present outcome.

The Weight of Inherited Consequences

People often ask:
"Why are we still dealing with this?"

The answer is simple and difficult:
Because we are still operating inside structures that were never dismantled—only renamed.

Structures do not require belief to function.
They require compliance.

And compliance is easiest when language explains harm as unfortunate rather than intentional.

Interrupting Memory

To interrupt a system's memory, three things must happen:

1. **The design must be named accurately**
   Not softened. Not abstracted.

2. **The outcomes must be traced to structure**
   Not redirected toward individuals.

3. **The logic must be changed**
   Not merely adjusted.

Language is essential at every stage.

Without naming, there is no target.
Without tracing, there is no accountability.
Without redesign, there is no change.

Closing Reflection (for the Reader)

Ask yourself:

- What systems in my life seem to "remember" harm?
- Where do I see patterns that persist despite good intentions?
- What explanations are offered instead of accountability?
- What would interruption—not reform—actually require?

Systems remember what people refuse to dismantle.

And forgetting, when it comes to design, is not innocence.

It is permission.

References (Chapter 5)

- Pierson, P. (2004). *Politics in Time: History, Institutions, and Social Analysis.*
- Bonilla-Silva, E. (2014). *Racism Without Racists.*
- Foucault, M. (1977). *Discipline and Punish.*
- Alexander, M. (2010). *The New Jim Crow.*
- Rothstein, R. (2017). *The Color of Law.*

Chapter 6
The Myth Of Personal Failure

Every system that harms people eventually learns the same trick.

It takes outcomes it produced
and reframes them as individual shortcomings.

When this happens, the system disappears from view—
and the person becomes the problem.

When Structure Becomes Character

Personal failure is one of the most effective myths ever created.

It sounds fair.
It sounds motivating.
It sounds like accountability.

But most of the time, it is **misdirected blame**.

When wages stagnate, people are told to "work harder."
When schools are underfunded, students are labeled "unmotivated."
When housing is inaccessible, families are called "irresponsible."
When care is unavailable, exhaustion is framed as weakness.

The system remains intact.
The individual absorbs the shame.

How Responsibility Was Reassigned

This shift did not happen accidentally.

In the late twentieth century, political and economic narratives increasingly emphasized **individual responsibility** while quietly withdrawing collective support (Harvey, 2005). Language followed policy.

Structural problems were reframed as:

- mindset issues
- work ethic gaps
- personal choices
- cultural flaws

This reframing served a purpose.
If failure is personal, then repair is private.
And systems are relieved of obligation.

"You Just Have to Work Harder"

Few phrases are more seductive—or more dangerous—than this one.

Hard work matters. Effort matters. Discipline matters.

But effort cannot compensate for **design**.

No amount of individual striving can:

- fix a predatory labor market
- fund an under-resourced school
- undo discriminatory lending
- replace missing healthcare
- restore stolen time

When hard work is presented as the solution to systemic harm, exhaustion becomes the price of survival—and burnout becomes a moral test.

Those who endure are praised.

Those who collapse are blamed.

Burnout Is Not Failure

Burnout is not a personal flaw.

It is a **signal**.

The World Health Organization Psychologists define burnout as chronic workplace stress that has not been successfully managed. It is not caused by laziness or lack of resilience—it is caused by prolonged exposure to unreasonable demands with insufficient support.

Yet burnout is often framed as:

- weakness
- lack of grit
- poor time management
- insufficient self-care

This framing again shifts responsibility away from systems and onto bodies.

The system demands more.
The person breaks.
And the break is treated as proof of inadequacy.

The Violence of Meritocracy

Meritocracy promises fairness.

If you work hard, you succeed.
If you fail, you didn't try hard enough.

But meritocracy only works when starting points are equal—and they are not.

Sociological research consistently shows that outcomes are strongly shaped by:

- family wealth
- neighborhood resources
- educational access
- racialized policy
- social networks

When these factors are ignored, meritocracy becomes a story people tell themselves to avoid confronting inequality.

Language keeps the myth alive.

Internalizing the System

When systems are blamed on individuals long enough, people begin to internalize the verdict.

They stop asking:

- What conditions shaped this outcome?
- Who designed this system?
- What alternatives exist?

And start asking:

- What's wrong with me?
- Why can't I keep up?
- Why am I failing?

This internalization is one of the most effective forms of control because it requires no external enforcement.

People regulate themselves.

Respectability as a Survival Strategy

In many marginalized communities, respectability became a shield.

Be perfect.
Be polite.
Be twice as good.
Don't complain.
Don't draw attention.

These strategies were rational responses to danger. They protected lives in hostile environments.

But when respectability becomes a requirement rather than a choice, it turns into a trap.

It asks people to absorb injustice quietly rather than challenge it openly.

And it reinforces the myth that success is simply a matter of behaving correctly.

Why Self-Blame Feels Safer Than System-Blame

Blaming oneself creates the illusion of control.

If the problem is me, then I can fix it.
If the problem is the system, then the task feels overwhelming.

Psychologists note that people often prefer self-blame over helplessness, even when self-blame is inaccurate. Language reflects this coping strategy.

But control built on false responsibility is fragile.

It collapses under pressure.

The Cost of Carrying What Was Never Yours

When individuals carry responsibility for systemic harm, the cost is not just emotional.

It shows up as:

- chronic stress
- anxiety
- depression
- disengagement
- shortened life expectancy

Public health research consistently links structural inequality to adverse health outcomes.

The body pays for the system's silence.

Reclaiming Accurate Responsibility

This chapter is not an invitation to abandon agency.

It is an invitation to **place agency where it belongs**.

Individuals matter.
Choices matter.
Effort matters.

But responsibility must be proportional to power.

Systems require collective action.

Design requires redesign.

Harm requires accountability.

Language that confuses these levels does violence quietly.

Closing Reflection (for the Reader)

Ask yourself:

- Where have I blamed myself for conditions I did not create?
- What expectations have I internalized that were not humane?
- Where might accurate language restore dignity rather than shame?
- What would change if failure were traced to design instead of character?

You were never meant to carry what an entire system produced.

And refusing that burden is not weakness.

It is clarity.

References (Chapter 6)

- Harvey, D. (2005). *A Brief History of Neoliberalism.*
- World Health Organization. (2019). *Burn-out an occupational phenomenon.*
- McNamee, S. J., & Miller, R. K. (2009). *The Meritocracy Myth.*
- Janoff-Bulman, R. (1979). *Characterological vs Behavioral Self-Blame.*
- Marmot, M. (2005). *Social Determinants of Health.*

Chapter 7
Breaking Generational Narratives

"This chapter is intentionally expansive. Generational narratives are among the most powerful carriers of language, shaping not only belief but identity, expectation, and belonging."

Every generation inherits a story.

Not just about who they are—but about what is possible for them.

These stories are rarely written down. They live in tone. In caution. In the phrases spoken when someone reaches too far, dreams too loudly, or asks for more than survival seems to allow.

They are not lies.
They are **responses to conditions**.

But responses, when left unexamined, become rules.

What a Generational Narrative Really Is

A generational narrative is not a myth or a slogan.
It is a **compressed lesson** passed down through repetition.

It answers questions before they are asked:

- How much should I expect?
- What happens if I challenge authority?
- What is realistic for someone like me?
- What must I endure quietly?

These narratives are not invented out of fear. They are forged in experience.

When danger is real, language becomes cautious.
When loss is frequent, hope becomes guarded.
When opportunity is scarce, ambition becomes suspicious.

This is not ignorance.
This is adaptation.

Survival Wisdom Has an Expiration Date

Survival language is brilliant at one thing: keeping people alive in hostile conditions.

But survival is not the same as living.

What protects one generation can confine the next.

- "Don't rock the boat."
- "Keep your head down."
- "Be grateful for what you get."
- "Don't expect too much."

These phrases once reduced risk.
Over time, they reduce possibility.

Honoring survival does not require freezing its language in place.

The Difference Between Loyalty and Repetition

Many people continue generational narratives out of loyalty.

To question the language feels like disrespect.
To rewrite it feels like betrayal.

But loyalty does not require imitation.

You can honor the past without reenacting its wounds.

In fact, refusing to repeat limiting narratives may be one of the highest forms of respect—because it acknowledges that earlier generations deserved better than what they were given.

They survived so someone else could thrive.

When Narrative Becomes Identity

The most powerful generational narratives do not sound like stories.

They sound like facts about *who we are.*

- "We always struggle."
- "We've never had it easy."
- "That's just how it is for us."

Over time, these phrases migrate from description to identity.

They stop referring to conditions and start defining people.

Sociological research shows that group narratives strongly influence collective behavior, aspiration, and tolerance for inequality (Somers). When struggle becomes identity, ease can feel unfamiliar—or even undeserved.

Breaking the narrative can feel like losing a part of oneself.

Why Breaking the Narrative Feels Risky

Breaking a generational narrative is not just an intellectual act. It is emotional. Social. Sometimes spiritual.

It can trigger:

- guilt
- fear of abandonment

- accusations of forgetting where you came from
- anxiety about standing alone

This is why narratives persist even when they cause harm.

Belonging often feels safer than freedom.

Liberation has never been an individual achievement. It is a collective process, and it frequently begins with a shift in how people speak, name, and understand their conditions.Choice Without Disrespect

Breaking generational narratives does not mean declaring them wrong.

It means asking:

- What conditions produced this belief?
- Does this still protect us?
- What does it cost us now?
- What must change for the next generation?

This is not rebellion for rebellion's sake.

It is **completion**.

Every generation is responsible for finishing the work its ancestors could not.

Language as a Site of Choice

You may not control the systems you inherit.
But you can choose the language you carry forward.

Choice begins when people recognize that:

- inherited does not mean inevitable
- tradition is not destiny

- survival is not the ceiling

Language is one of the few places where change is immediately available.

Not because words are magical—but because they influence attention, expectation, and action.

From "This Is How It Is" to "This Is How It's Been"

One of the most powerful shifts is grammatical.

"This is how it is" closes the future.
"This is how it's been" opens it.

The difference is subtle—and revolutionary.

It acknowledges reality without surrendering to it.

Making Space for What Was Never Modeled

For many people, these experiences were never modeled:

- rest without guilt
- wealth without exploitation
- leadership without burnout
- care without scarcity

This absence shapes what feels imaginable—and what does not.

Without models, imagination feels unsafe.

This is why breaking narratives requires patience. People are not resisting change—they are protecting themselves from disappointment.

But protection is not the same as truth.

The Responsibility of the Present Generation

Every generation stands at a crossroads.

It can repeat what it was given.
Or it can revise it.

Revising does not erase history.
It reorients it.

You are not responsible for what was inherited.
You are responsible for what is transmitted next.

Closing Reflection (for the Reader)

Ask yourself:

- What narratives did I inherit about struggle, success, or worth?
- Which ones protected my ancestors?
- Which ones are limiting me now?
- What language would allow the next generation more room to breathe?

Breaking generational narratives is not rejection.

It is an act of care.

And care, when practiced intentionally, becomes liberation.

References (Chapter 7)

- Somers, M. (1994). *The Narrative Constitution of Identity.*
- Freire, P. (1970). *Pedagogy of the Oppressed.*

- hooks, b. (1994). *Teaching to Transgress.*
- Brave Heart, M. Y. H. (1998). *Historical Trauma.*
- Alexander, M. (2010). *The New Jim Crow.*

Chapter 8
Words, Power, And The Body

Language does not land only in the mind.
It lands in the body first.

Before a word becomes an idea, it becomes a sensation.
A tightening.
A brace.
A release.
A familiar sinking feeling.

This is why some phrases feel heavy before we understand why.
The body remembers what the mouth repeats.

Trauma Is a Pattern of Anticipation

Trauma is not only what happened.
It is what the body expects next.

Neuroscience research shows that repeated exposure to stress conditions the nervous system to anticipate threat, scarcity, or disappointment—even in environments that are objectively neutral. Scholars such as Bessel van der Kolk and Stephen Porges have demonstrated how chronic stress reshapes physiological responses, narrowing a person's sense of safety and possibility.

Language plays a key role in this anticipation.

Phrases like:

- "Don't get your hopes up."
- "Something always goes wrong."
- "You know how it is."

prepare the body to brace.

This is not pessimism.
It is **protection**.

But protection, when prolonged, becomes limitation.

How Language Trains the Nervous System

The nervous system learns through repetition.

When language repeatedly signals danger, futility, or inevitability, the body adapts accordingly:

- muscles tense
- breath shortens
- attention narrows
- imagination contracts

This state is efficient for survival—but costly for creativity, connection, and long-term planning.

Polyvagal theory explains that people cannot access higher-order thinking or relational engagement when their nervous systems are stuck in defense

In other words:
You cannot imagine liberation while bracing for harm.

Why "Positive Thinking" Fails

Many responses to limiting language focus on positivity.

Think better thoughts.
Speak abundance.
Manifest success.

But positivity without regulation can feel dishonest—or even dangerous—to a traumatized nervous system.

The body knows when language doesn't match reality.

When people are told to "just think positive" while still navigating structural harm, the nervous system experiences dissonance rather than relief.

This is why affirmation without accuracy often backfires.

Healing does not begin with optimism.
It begins with **safety and truth**.

Regulation Before Reimagination

Liberation requires imagination—but imagination requires regulation.

A regulated nervous system can:

- tolerate uncertainty
- consider alternatives
- take measured risks
- remain present without shutting down

Language that acknowledges harm *without normalizing it* helps create this regulation.

For example:

- "This is difficult" instead of "this is impossible"
- "This has been harmful" instead of "this is just how it is"
- "This needs to change" instead of "nothing ever changes"

Precision calms the body.

Power Speaks to the Body First

Power rarely announces itself with force alone.

It whispers:

- "Don't push too hard."
- "Be realistic."
- "Know your place."
- "Be grateful."

These messages are not abstract. They land somatically.

Sociologist Michel Foucault noted that power disciplines bodies long before it persuades minds (Foucault, 1977). Language is one of its most effective tools.

The body learns where not to go—before the mind catches up.

Chronic Stress and Narrowed Futures

Public health research links chronic stress to reduced life expectancy, cognitive load, and emotional exhaustion (Marmot, 2005).

When language continually reinforces scarcity, urgency, or futility, it keeps people in a constant state of readiness.

This readiness is exhausting.

And exhaustion makes people easier to manage.

A tired body does not organize.
A braced body does not imagine.
A depleted body does not demand better.

Reclaiming the Body Through Language

Language can also do the opposite.

It can:

- slow the breath
- widen attention
- restore choice
- signal safety

This is why trauma-informed facilitation prioritizes:

- clarity over intensity
- choice over coercion
- accuracy over optimism

Language that names harm precisely—without dramatizing it—helps the body orient to reality instead of threat.

From Survival Speech to Regulated Speech

Survival speech moves quickly.
It compresses.
It avoids risk.

Regulated speech allows pause.

It sounds like:

- "Let's slow this down."
- "We don't have to decide right now."
- "This deserves careful thought."
- "This isn't inevitable."

These phrases do not deny difficulty.

They create space inside it.

The Body as a Site of Liberation

Liberation is not only political.

It is physiological.

A body that remains in a state of bracing is unable to access freedom, even when exposed to transformative ideas. For this reason, language work must be trauma-informed—not because people lack resilience, but because lived histories shape nervous system responses. Restoring agency requires language that also helps restore regulation..

Closing Reflection (for the Reader)

Notice your body as you read these words.

- Which phrases make you tense?
- Which ones soften your breath?
- Which language signals safety?
- Which language signals danger?

Your body is not overreacting.
It is remembering.

And remembering, when honored, becomes the foundation for change.

References (Chapter 8)

- van der Kolk, B. (2014). *The Body Keeps the Score.*
- Porges, S. (2011). *The Polyvagal Theory.*

- McEwen, B. (1998). *Protective and Damaging Effects of Stress.*
- Marmot, M. (2005). *Social Determinants of Health.*
- Foucault, M. (1977). *Discipline and Punish.*

Chapter 9
The Violence Of Small Phrases

Not all violence leaves bruises.

Some of it arrives as advice.
Some of it sounds like wisdom.
Some of it is repeated with love.

Small phrases—spoken casually, inherited uncritically, repeated endlessly—can carry immense power. Not because they are dramatic, but because they are *ordinary*. They slip past resistance. They shape belief quietly.

This is how harm becomes familiar.

Why Small Phrases Matter

Large declarations are easier to challenge.

Small phrases are harder.

They arrive in moments of vulnerability:

- when someone is tired
- when hope feels risky
- when disappointment feels inevitable

They are offered as comfort:

- "Don't get your hopes up."
- "It wasn't meant for us."
- "That's just how it is."

These phrases are rarely malicious. They are attempts to soften pain.

But comfort that requires resignation has a cost.

When Advice Becomes Limitation

Advice often reflects past conditions.

What kept someone safe in one era may confine someone else in another.

Phrases like:

- "Keep your head down."
- "Don't rock the boat."
- "Be grateful for what you get."

once reduced risk. They taught caution in dangerous environments.

But when danger changes—or when people seek transformation rather than survival—these same phrases become barriers.

They teach compliance when disruption is needed.

The Cumulative Effect of Repetition

No single phrase determines a life.

But language works cumulatively.

When limiting phrases are repeated:

- expectations shrink
- risk feels irresponsible
- ambition feels naive
- rest feels undeserved

Cognitive psychology confirms that repeated messaging influences perception and behavior, even when individuals consciously reject it (Bargh, 1997).

The harm is not in one sentence.
It is in the **ecosystem of speech**.

Language as a Tool of Containment

Systems do not need censorship when people censor themselves.

When language repeatedly frames struggle as normal, ambition as dangerous, or comfort as unrealistic, people learn to manage their desires accordingly.

This is containment without force.

Sociologist Antonio Gramsci called this *hegemony*—when dominant ideas become common sense, and resistance begins to feel unreasonable (Gramsci, 1971).

Small phrases are often the delivery system.

Familiar Phrases, Familiar Outcomes

Consider how these phrases function:

- "We don't get nice things."
  → Lowers expectations for quality, care, and beauty.
- "You gotta be twice as good."
  → Normalizes overwork and exhaustion.
- "Money changes people."
  → Frames wealth as moral danger.
- "That's just how it is."
  → Ends inquiry and accountability.

Each phrase carries an instruction.

Not explicit—but effective.

Why Intention Does Not Cancel Impact

Many people resist examining these phrases because they were spoken with love.

But intention does not determine impact.

Trauma research emphasizes that harm can occur without malicious intent, especially when messages are repeated during formative moments (Herman, 1992).

Language learned early, under stress, or from trusted figures carries disproportionate weight.

This does not make elders wrong.
It makes context essential.

The Trap of Cultural Romanticization

There is a temptation to protect all inherited language as sacred.

But culture is not static. It is living.

Romanticizing survival language without questioning its current function risks preserving the very conditions it once helped navigate.

Audre Lorde warned that survival strategies should not be mistaken for liberation (Lorde, 1984).

Language that once kept people alive may no longer be enough.

Precision as a Form of Care

Challenging small phrases is not about correction.

It is about **care**.

Care for:

- truth
- clarity
- future generations
- emotional health

Precision allows people to locate responsibility accurately.

Instead of:

- "People just don't want to work"
  we can say:
- "Wages no longer support basic living."

Instead of:

- "It's always been this way"
  we can say:
- "This was designed and can be redesigned."

Precision does not remove empathy.
It strengthens it.

Rewriting Without Erasing

This work is not about banning phrases.

It is about expanding them.

Not:

- "We've always struggled."
  But:
- "We've struggled—and we deserve ease."

Not:

- "This world doesn't owe us anything."
  But:
- "Dignity is not something we earn."

Language can evolve without losing its roots.

Small Shifts, Real Consequences

Changing how people speak does not immediately change systems.

But it changes:

- what they notice
- what they tolerate
- what they demand
- what they organize around

Systems rely on predictable language.

When language shifts, predictability weakens.

And weakened predictability creates opportunity.

Closing Reflection (for the Reader)

Listen closely to the phrases that surround you.

- Which ones lower expectations?

- Which ones discourage action?
- Which ones sound wise but feel heavy?
- Which ones deserve context—or retirement?

Not every familiar phrase deserves permanence.

Some are meant to be questioned.
Some are meant to be revised.
Some are meant to be released.

Small phrases can do great harm.

They can also be where liberation begins.

References (Chapter 9)

- Bargh, J. A. (1997). *The Automaticity of Everyday Life.*
- Herman, J. (1992). *Trauma and Recovery.*
- Gramsci, A. (1971). *Selections from the Prison Notebooks.*
- Lorde, A. (1984). *Sister Outsider.*
- Lakoff, G. (2004). *Don't Think of an Elephant.*

Chapter 10
Redefining Luxury

Luxury has not simply been misunderstood; it has been strategically reframed. By associating luxury with indulgence, excess, and moral irresponsibility, it has been positioned as inappropriate—especially for communities whose survival has been repeatedly politicized and scrutinized.

But luxury, at its core, has never been about things.

It has always been about **conditions**.

How Luxury Was Stolen and Rebranded

Luxury was not originally synonymous with waste.

Historically, luxury referred to:

- time to rest
- access to beauty
- safety from harm
- freedom from constant urgency
- the ability to live without perpetual fear

Over time, as systems of extraction and inequality expanded, luxury was rebranded as:

- exclusivity
- status signaling
- consumption without responsibility

And then something more insidious happened.

Marginalized people were taught that luxury was not for them.

When Survival Becomes a Moral Identity

In many communities, struggle became proof of character.

Working hard became virtuous.
Endurance became admirable.
Rest became suspicious.

Luxury, meanwhile, was framed as:

- irresponsible

- unserious

- unattainable

- dangerous

This framing did not emerge naturally. It was taught.

Sociologists have observed that societies often moralize deprivation in order to justify unequal distribution of resources. When people are taught that suffering builds character, systems are quietly relieved of the responsibility to reduce suffering. Struggle becomes a badge.
Ease becomes a threat.

The Psychological Cost of Denying Ease

When people are conditioned to believe that comfort is undeserved, they learn to distrust peace.

Moments of rest trigger guilt.
Periods of stability feel temporary.

Pleasure feels borrowed.
This is not personal dysfunction.
It is cultural conditioning.

Trauma research shows that people exposed to chronic stress often experience difficulty tolerating calm, because calm feels unfamiliar or unsafe (van der Kolk, 2014).

Luxury, in this sense, is not excess—it is **regulation**.

Luxury as Regulation, Not Indulgence

A regulated life includes:

- predictable rest
- emotional safety
- time to think
- space to imagine
- freedom from constant crisis

These are not rewards for good behavior.
They are prerequisites for health, creativity, and civic engagement.

Public health research consistently links stability and access to resources with better outcomes across education, health, and community participation (Marmot, 2005).

Luxury is not the opposite of responsibility.
It is what makes responsibility sustainable.

Who Decides What Is "Too Much"?

Luxury often becomes controversial only when it is claimed by people who were expected to have access to it.
When marginalized communities seek:

- quality
- beauty

- ease
- abundance

those desires are frequently reframed as excess rather than entitlement.

But when these same things are hoarded elsewhere, they are called success.

This double standard reveals the truth: luxury is political.

Who is allowed comfort?
Who must justify rest?
Who is expected to endure?

These are not neutral questions.

Redefining Wealth Beyond Survival

Wealth is often reduced to money.

But real wealth includes:

- time sovereignty
- bodily safety
- emotional capacity
- access to care
- freedom from constant stress

Economists have long argued that wealth should be measured not only by income, but by quality of life and opportunity (Sen).

A life organized around constant survival is not poor because of mindset.
It is poor because systems withhold resources.

Luxury is the opposite of that withholding.

Why Wanting More Is Not Greed

Greed is accumulation without regard for harm.

Wanting:

- rest
- dignity
- stability
- beauty
- joy

is not greed.

It is a refusal to accept deprivation as normal.

When people are taught to distrust their desire for more, they are easier to manage. Desire, when suppressed, does not disappear— it turns inward as shame.

Reclaiming luxury is reclaiming permission.

Luxury as a Collective Concept

True luxury is not individual escape.

It is collective conditions.

A community where:

- care is accessible
- labor is valued
- rest is normalized
- safety is expected
- creativity is supported

This is not fantasy.

It is design.

And design can be changed.

From Scarcity Thinking to Abundance Thinking— Carefully

This book does not advocate denial of reality.

Scarcity exists.
Inequality is real.
Resources are unevenly distributed.

But scarcity thinking becomes dangerous when it is treated as permanent.

Abundance is not pretending resources are infinite.
It is insisting they be distributed justly.

Luxury, in this sense, is ethical.

Reclaiming Luxury Without Apology

There is nothing radical about wanting a life that is:

- peaceful
- prosperous
- well-resourced
- joyful
- free from constant crisis

What is radical is how often people are taught to apologize for wanting these things.

Luxury is not the enemy of liberation.

It is evidence of it.

Closing Reflection (for the Reader)

Ask yourself:

- What has luxury been defined as in my life?
- When did I learn that ease was suspicious?
- What conditions would allow me to live with dignity rather than endurance?
- What would it mean to stop apologizing for wanting more than survival?

Luxury is not a distraction from justice.

It is one of its outcomes.

References (Chapter 10)

- Gans, H. J. (1995). *The War Against the Poor.*
- van der Kolk, B. (2014). *The Body Keeps the Score.*
- Marmot, M. (2005). *Social Determinants of Health.*
- Sen, A. (1999). *Development as Freedom.*

hooks, b. (2000). *All About Love.*

Chapter 11
Sovereignty Is A Language Practice

Sovereignty is often imagined as something dramatic.

A declaration.
A revolution.
A moment when power shifts visibly.

But most sovereignty begins much earlier—and much quieter than that.

It begins in how people speak about themselves, their conditions, and their possibilities.

What Sovereignty Actually Means

Sovereignty is not domination.
It is not isolation.
It is not control over others.

Sovereignty is **self-governance**—the ability to act with agency, clarity, and consent within systems that were not designed for you.

It is the difference between reacting and choosing.
Between enduring and directing.

And language is one of the primary tools through which sovereignty is practiced—or surrendered.

How Language Trains Agency

Agency does not emerge from willpower alone.

It emerges from **accurate language**.

When people repeatedly describe their lives using language that:

- minimizes harm
- normalizes scarcity
- frames struggle as identity

they quietly train themselves to expect less influence over outcomes.

Conversely, language that:

- names systems
- distinguishes conditions from character
- frames struggle as contextual rather than personal

supports agency without denial.

This is not positive thinking.
It is **accurate thinking**.

Precision Over Slogans

Slogans feel powerful because they are simple.

But simplicity without accuracy creates illusion.

Sovereignty requires precision.

Consider the difference between:

- "I'm bad with money"
  and
- "I was never taught financial systems designed to benefit me."

One collapses responsibility inward.
The other locates responsibility where it belongs—while still leaving room for learning.

74

Precision restores choice.

Speaking Without Permission

One of the quiet losses of systemic harm is permission.

People learn:

- when to speak
- how much to say
- what not to name
- what to soften

This self-censorship often masquerades as maturity or professionalism.

But sovereignty requires **truthful speech**, not reckless speech.

Truthful speech:

- names harm without spectacle
- names desire without apology
- names limits without shame

This kind of language disrupts power not by force, but by clarity.

The Relationship Between Language and Boundaries

Boundaries are not only behavioral.

They are linguistic.

People who lack language for boundaries often struggle to enforce them.

Phrases like:

- "I'm fine"

- "It's not that serious"
- "I don't want to make a fuss"

may feel polite—but they erase needs.

Trauma-informed research shows that clear language supports nervous system regulation and relational safety (Siegel, 2010).

Sovereignty requires the ability to name limits without justification.

Why Sovereignty Feels Uncomfortable at First

For many people, sovereignty feels unfamiliar.

It can trigger:

- guilt
- fear of backlash
- accusations of selfishness
- internalized doubt

This is not because sovereignty is wrong.

It is because systems depend on people who self-limit.

When someone begins to speak differently—more precisely, more calmly, more clearly—it disrupts expectations.

Silence feels safer.
Precision feels risky.

But risk is often the cost of agency.

Language as Daily Practice, Not Performance

Sovereignty is not something you announce.

It is something you practice.

It shows up in:

- how you describe your work
- how you explain your needs
- how you narrate setbacks
- how you frame possibility

It does not require grand speeches.

It requires consistency.

From Reaction to Direction

Reaction is shaped by urgency.
Direction is shaped by intention.

Language that constantly reinforces urgency keeps people reacting.

Language that allows pause creates space for strategy.

Phrases like:

- "Let's assess this."
- "This deserves consideration."
- "We don't need to decide immediately."

are acts of sovereignty.

They slow the pace of extraction.

Sovereignty Is Collective

Individual sovereignty matters.

But collective sovereignty is transformative.

When communities share language that:

- names systems
- resists resignation
- normalizes care
- expects dignity

they become harder to exploit.

Shared language creates shared reality.

And shared reality is the foundation of collective power.

Practicing Sovereignty in an Unsupportive World

This book does not pretend the world is fair.

Systems still exist.
Harm still occurs.
Resources remain unequal.

Sovereignty does not eliminate these realities.

It equips people to navigate them without surrendering identity or dignity.

It is not escape.

It is orientation.

Closing Reflection (for the Reader)

Ask yourself:

- Where does my language shrink me?
- Where does it protect me?
- Where does it locate responsibility inaccurately?
- What would it sound like to speak with clarity rather than apology?

Sovereignty is not something you wait for.

It is something you practice—sentence by sentence.

References (Chapter 11)

- Siegel, D. J. (2010). *The Mindful Brain.*
- Freire, P. (1970). *Pedagogy of the Oppressed.*
- hooks, b. (1994). *Teaching to Transgress.*
- Foucault, M. (1977). *Discipline and Punish.*
- Sen, A. (1999). *Development as Freedom.*

Chapter 12
From Consciousness To Action

Awareness is not the destination.

It is the beginning.

Too many people mistake understanding for transformation. They learn the language of systems, name the harm, recognize the patterns—and stop there. But systems are not disrupted by insight alone. They are disrupted by **sustained, coordinated action** rooted in clarity.

This chapter exists to make one thing unmistakable:
liberation is not an idea—it is a practice.

Consciousness Without Action Is a Luxury of Its Own

There is a quiet danger in awareness without movement.

It can become:

- performance
- identity
- superiority
- despair disguised as realism

Critical consciousness, as Paulo Freire warned, is incomplete without praxis—reflection *and* action. To see the system clearly but refuse to engage it is to turn knowledge into a kind of isolation.

Understanding is not meant to make you comfortable.
It is meant to make you responsible.

What Action Actually Looks Like

Action does not always look dramatic.

Most of the work that changes systems looks ordinary:

- organizing meetings
- asking better questions
- refusing harmful narratives
- designing alternatives
- protecting care
- sustaining pressure

Action is often quiet, repetitive, and unglamorous.

And that is why it works.

Language as Civic Engagement

Language is one of the first sites of civic participation.

Every time people:

- name a system instead of blaming themselves
- question inevitability
- demand clarity
- refuse resignation

they are participating in democracy.

Civic engagement is not limited to voting or protest. It includes how people talk about:

- policy
- labor

- education
- care
- worth

Words shape what becomes politically imaginable.

Interrupting Systems Requires Collective Will

No one interrupts a system alone.

Systems are collective structures.
They require collective responses.

This is why shared language matters.

When communities agree on:

- what the problem actually is
- who holds responsibility
- what outcomes are unacceptable

coordination becomes possible.

Without shared language, action fragments.
With it, movement becomes sustainable.

Refusing Despair as an Identity

Despair often presents itself as realism.

"I see the system. I know how it works. Nothing will change."

But despair is not wisdom.

It is exhaustion looking for rest.

Refusing despair does not mean denying difficulty. It means refusing to let difficulty become destiny.

Systems depend on people giving up emotionally long before they give up materially.

Hope, in this sense, is not optimism.

It is endurance with direction.

What This Book Is—and Is Not—Asking

This book is not asking you to:

- save everyone
- be perfect
- fix everything
- burn yourself out
- carry what systems created

It *is* asking you to:

- speak accurately
- locate responsibility correctly
- protect your capacity
- practice care strategically
- refuse normalization of harm

Liberation is not martyrdom.

Sustainability is ethical.

The Role of Luxury in Action

Luxury—redefined as care, peace, dignity, and access—is not a distraction from justice.

It is what allows justice work to continue.

A burned-out movement collapses.
A regulated one endures.

Action without care reproduces the very harm it seeks to dismantle.

This is why luxury belongs in liberation work.

Not as indulgence—but as infrastructure.

Passing the Language Forward

Every generation leaves something behind.

Not just systems—but stories.

Not just policies—but phrases.

The question is not whether language will be inherited.

It is **what kind**.

Will it be language that:

- normalizes harm?
- romanticizes struggle?
- excuses inequality?

Or language that:

- names systems?
- expects dignity?
- protects care?
- insists on possibility?

The future is trained in the present.

A Final Invitation

This book is not a prophecy.

It is a map.

It does not promise ease.
It promises clarity.

And clarity is powerful.

You are not powerless because systems exist.
You are powerful when you understand how they work—and choose to act anyway.

Sentence by sentence.
Choice by choice.
Together.

Closing Reflection (for the Reader)

Ask yourself:

- What language will I no longer carry?
- What language will I practice instead?
- Where can my clarity support collective action?
- What does sustainable liberation look like in my life?

You were not meant to live forever in survival mode.

You were meant to live with dignity, care, and agency.

That life is not imaginary.

It is built.

References (Chapter 12)

- Freire, P. (1970). *Pedagogy of the Oppressed.*
- hooks, b. (2000). *All About Love.*
- Sen, A. (1999). *Development as Freedom.*
- Ostrom, E. (2010). *Beyond Markets and States.*
- Kelley, R. D. G. (2002). *Freedom Dreams.*

A Letter for the Road

If you've reached this point, you already know something important:

The way we speak is not accidental.

It is shaped.
It is taught.
And it can be changed.

You are not responsible for the language you inherited.
But you are responsible for what you pass forward.

May you speak with clarity instead of resignation.
May you name systems instead of blaming yourself.
May you protect your capacity for care.
May you insist on dignity without apology.

Luxury—true luxury—is not excess.
It is a life no longer organized around survival.

That life is not imaginary.
It is designed.

And design can be changed.

— *Luxorae*

Bibliography

Alexander, M. (2010). *The New Jim Crow.*

Arendt, H. (1963). *Eichmann in Jerusalem.*

Bandura, A. (1999). Moral disengagement in the perpetration of inhumanities.

Bargh, J. A. (1997). The automaticity of everyday life.

Bonilla-Silva, E. (2014). *Racism Without Racists.*

Bourdieu, P. (1984). *Distinction.*

Bourdieu, P. (1991). *Language and Symbolic Power.*

Freire, P. (1970). *Pedagogy of the Oppressed.*

Gans, H. J. (1995). *The War Against the Poor.*

Gramsci, A. (1971). *Prison Notebooks.*

Harvey, D. (2005). *A Brief History of Neoliberalism.*

Hasher, L., Goldstein, D., & Toppino, T. (1977). Frequency and truth.

Herman, J. (1992). *Trauma and Recovery.*

hooks, b. (1994). *Teaching to Transgress.*

hooks, b. (2000). *All About Love.*

Hochschild, A. (1983). *The Managed Heart.*

Kelley, R. D. G. (2002). *Freedom Dreams.*

Lakoff, G. (2004). *Don't Think of an Elephant.*

Lakoff, G., & Johnson, M. (1980). *Metaphors We Live By.*

Marmot, M. (2005). Social determinants of health.

McEwen, B. (1998). Stress and the brain.

McNamee, S. J., & Miller, R. K. (2009). *The Meritocracy Myth.*

Ostrom, E. (2010). Beyond markets and states.

Pierson, P. (2004). *Politics in Time.*

Porges, S. (2011). *The Polyvagal Theory.*

Rothstein, R. (2017). *The Color of Law.*

Scott, J. C. (1990). *Domination and the Arts of Resistance.*

Sen, A. (1999). *Development as Freedom.*

Siegel, D. J. (2010). *The Mindful Brain.*

Somers, M. (1994). Narrative identity.

van der Kolk, B. (2014). *The Body Keeps the Score.*

World Health Organization. (2019). Burnout classification.